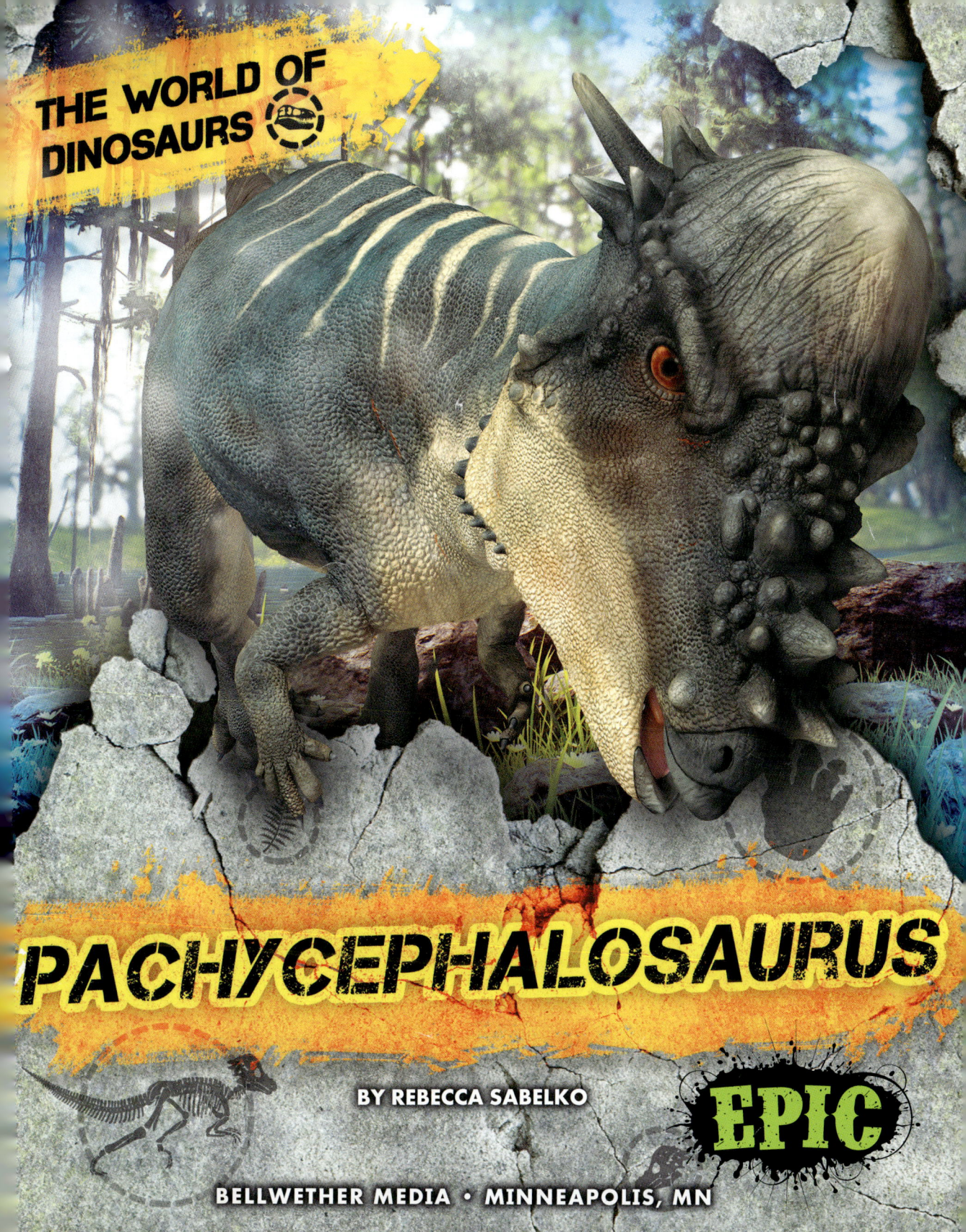
THE WORLD OF DINOSAURS

PACHYCEPHALOSAURUS

BY REBECCA SABELKO

EPIC

BELLWETHER MEDIA • MINNEAPOLIS, MN

EPIC

EPIC BOOKS are no ordinary books. They burst with intense action, high-speed heroics, and shadows of the unknown. Are you ready for an Epic adventure?

This edition first published in 2024 by Bellwether Media, Inc.

No part of this publication may be reproduced in whole or in part without written permission of the publisher. For information regarding permission, write to Bellwether Media, Inc., Attention: Permissions Department, 6012 Blue Circle Drive, Minnetonka, MN 55343.

Library of Congress Cataloging-in-Publication Data

Names: Sabelko, Rebecca, author.
Title: Pachycephalosaurus / by Rebecca Sabelko.
Description: Minneapolis, MN : Bellwether Media, 2024. | Series: The world of dinosaurs |
  Includes bibliographical references and index. | Audience: Ages 7-12 | Audience: Grades 4-6 |
  Summary: "Engaging images accompany information about the pachycephalosaurus. The combination
  of high-interest subject matter and light text is intended for students in grades 2 through 7"--
  Provided by publisher.
Identifiers: LCCN 2023020261 (print) | LCCN 2023020262 (ebook) | ISBN 9798886875041
  (library binding) | ISBN 9798886875546 (paperback) | ISBN 9798886876925 (ebook)
Subjects: LCSH: Pachycephalosaurus--Juvenile literature.
Classification: LCC QE862.O65 S2388 2024 (print) | LCC QE862.O65 (ebook) |
  DDC 567.914--dc23/eng/20230512
LC record available at https://lccn.loc.gov/2023020261
LC ebook record available at https://lccn.loc.gov/2023020262

Text copyright © 2024 by Bellwether Media, Inc. EPIC and associated logos are trademarks and/or registered trademarks of Bellwether Media, Inc.

Editor: Rachael Barnes   Designer: Jeffrey Kollock

Printed in the United States of America, North Mankato, MN.

TABLE OF CONTENTS

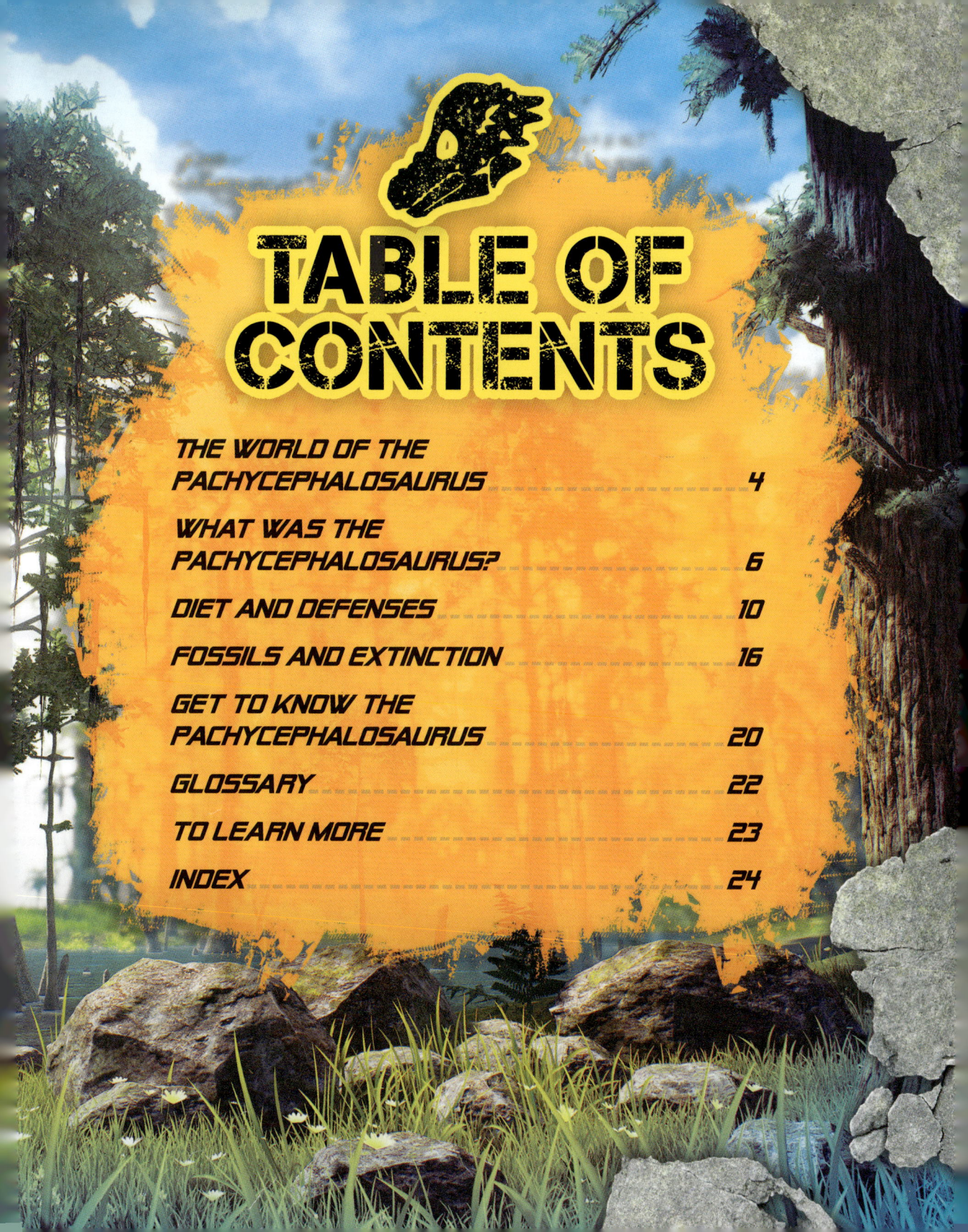

THE WORLD OF THE PACHYCEPHALOSAURUS	4
WHAT WAS THE PACHYCEPHALOSAURUS?	6
DIET AND DEFENSES	10
FOSSILS AND EXTINCTION	16
GET TO KNOW THE PACHYCEPHALOSAURUS	20
GLOSSARY	22
TO LEARN MORE	23
INDEX	24

THE WORLD OF THE PACHYCEPHALOSAURUS

PRONUNCIATION

PAK-ee-SEF-a-loh-SORE-us

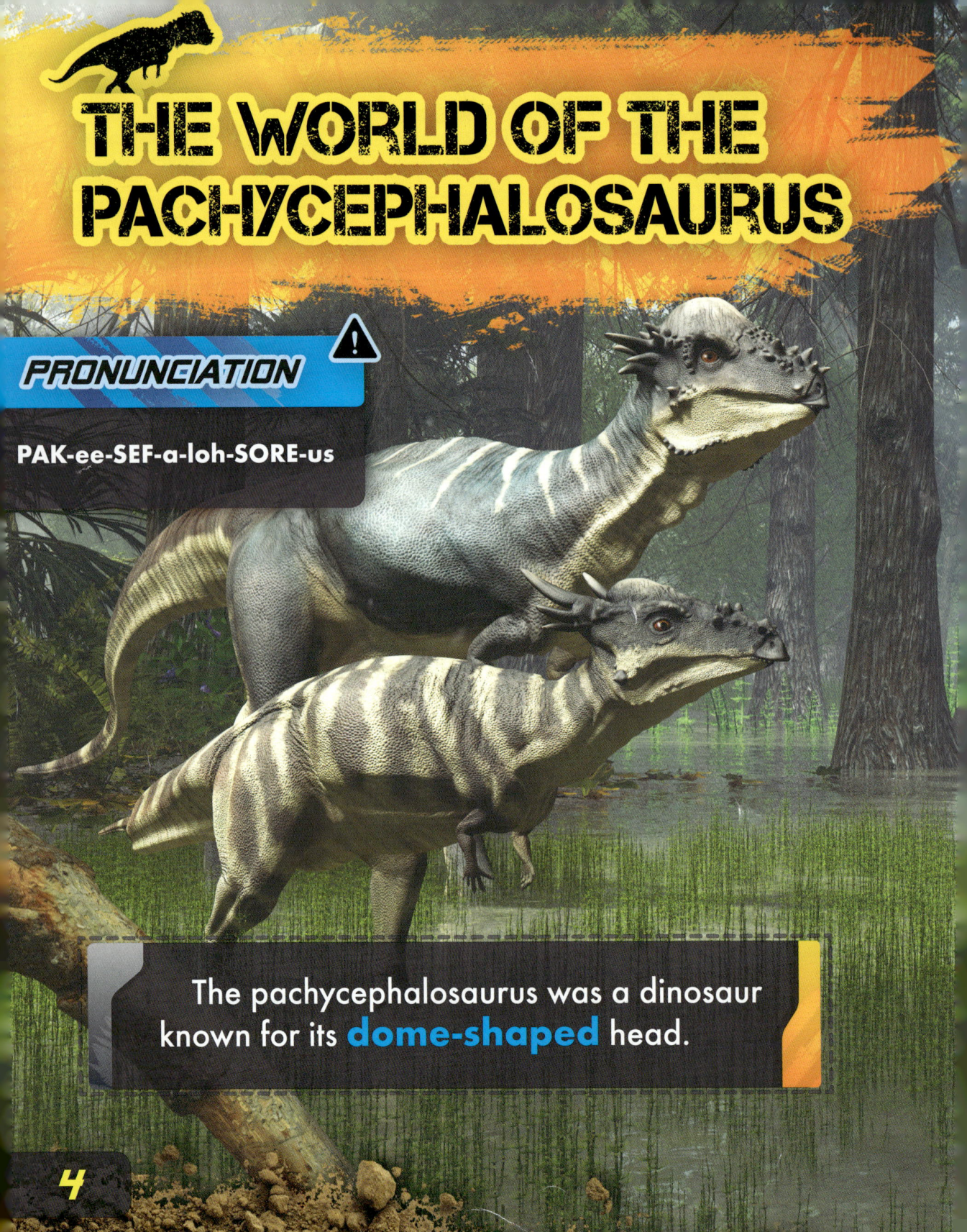

The pachycephalosaurus was a dinosaur known for its **dome-shaped** head.

4

MAP OF THE WORLD

Late Cretaceous period

NAME GAME

The name *pachycephalosaurus* means "thick-headed lizard."

It lived around 70 million years ago. This was during the Late **Cretaceous period** of the **Mesozoic era**.

WHAT WAS THE PACHYCEPHALOSAURUS?

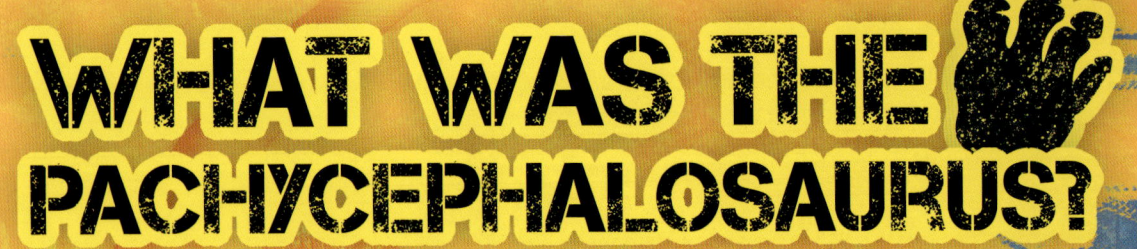

rounded spikes

The pachycephalosaurus's dome was big. It reached up to 10 inches (25 centimeters) thick!

Rounded spikes stuck up around the dome. They also ran down the dinosaur's nose.

HEADBUTTING

Scientists once thought pachycephalosaurses used their thick domes to headbutt in fights. Today, many believe the dinosaur's dome was not strong enough.

This dinosaur reached around 15 feet (5 meters) long. It weighed up to 1,000 pounds (454 kilograms).

The dinosaur had two short arms. It moved on its two strong back legs.

FLAT HEADS

Fossils of young show that the pachycephalosaurus likely did not grow a dome until it was an adult.

SIZE CHART

15 feet (4.6 meters)

10 feet (3 meters)

5 feet (1.5 meters)

DIET AND DEFENSES

beak

The pachycephalosaurus mostly ate plants. It also ate seeds.

It snapped leaves from stems with its hard beak. It used its flat back teeth to **grind** tough food.

⚠ PACHYCEPHALOSAURUS DIET

seeds

leafy plants

lizards

11

This dinosaur's front teeth were sharp! They were shaped like blades.

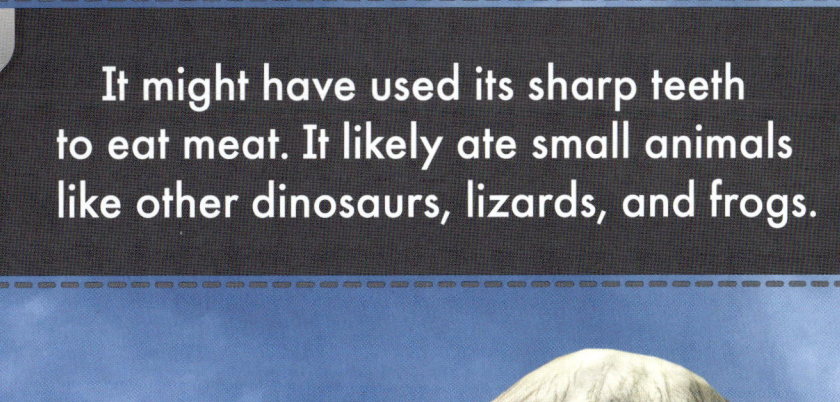

It might have used its sharp teeth to eat meat. It likely ate small animals like other dinosaurs, lizards, and frogs.

It was likely hunted by large **predators**. It shared a **habitat** with the Tyrannosaurus rex.

14

Tyrannosaurus rex

The pachycephalosaurus had large, front-facing eyes. These helped the dinosaur see predators coming from far away.

FOSSILS AND EXTINCTION

asteroid

16

A huge **asteroid** hit Earth about 66 million years ago. It changed habitats around the world.

The pachycephalosaurus could not survive the changes. It died out.

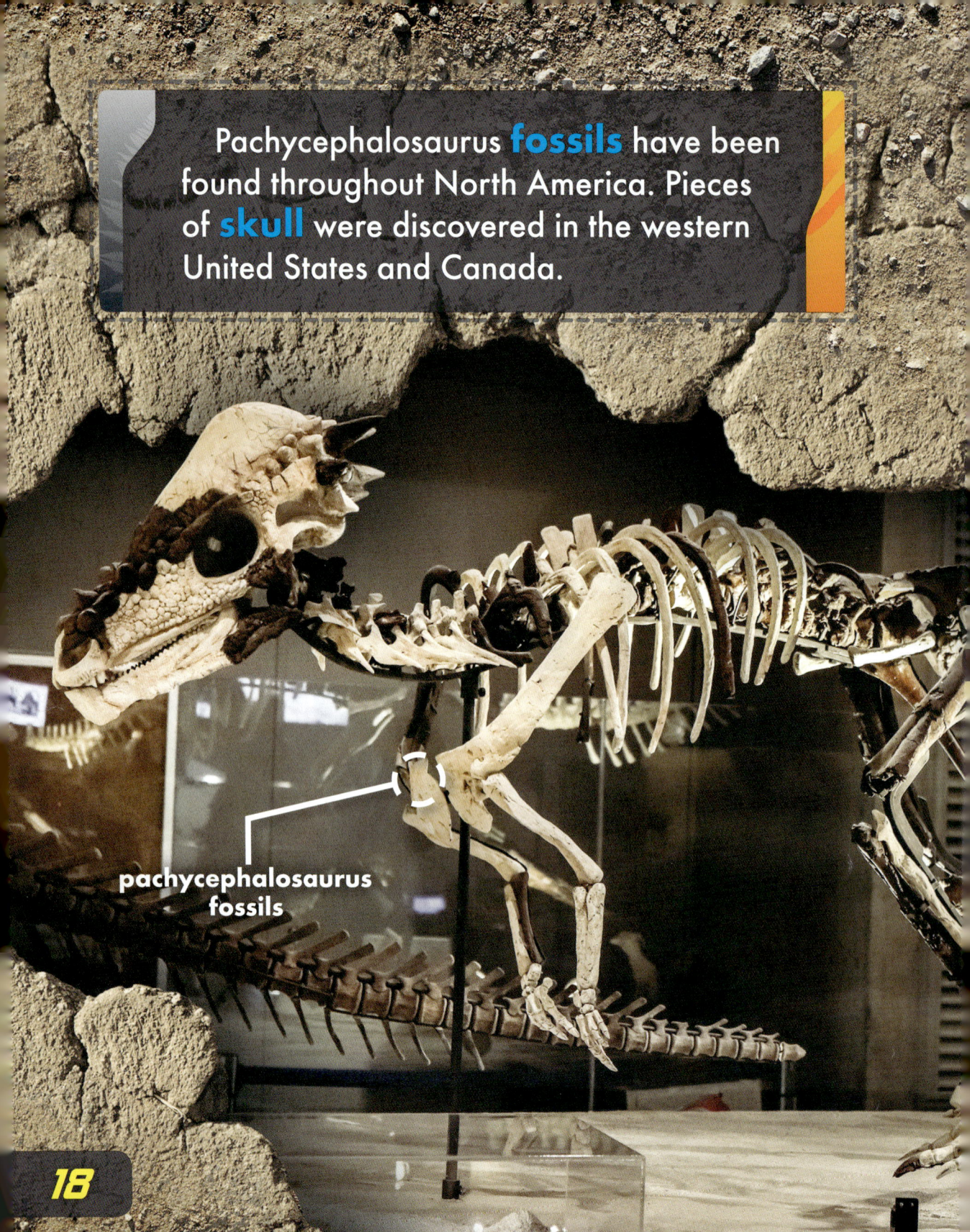

Pachycephalosaurus **fossils** have been found throughout North America. Pieces of **skull** were discovered in the western United States and Canada.

pachycephalosaurus fossils

GET TO KNOW THE PACHYCEPHALOSAURUS

dome-shaped head

FIRST FOSSILS FOUND
Lance and Hell Creek Formations, Montana, around 1860

rounded spikes

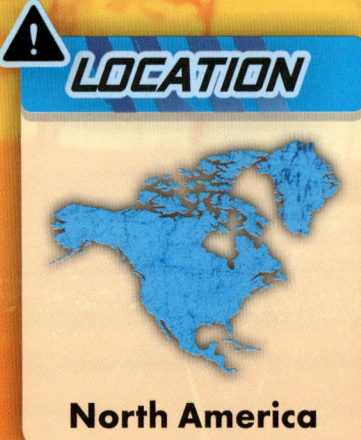
LOCATION
North America

short arms

HEIGHT up to 6 feet (2 meters)

LENGTH around 15 feet (5 meters) long

20

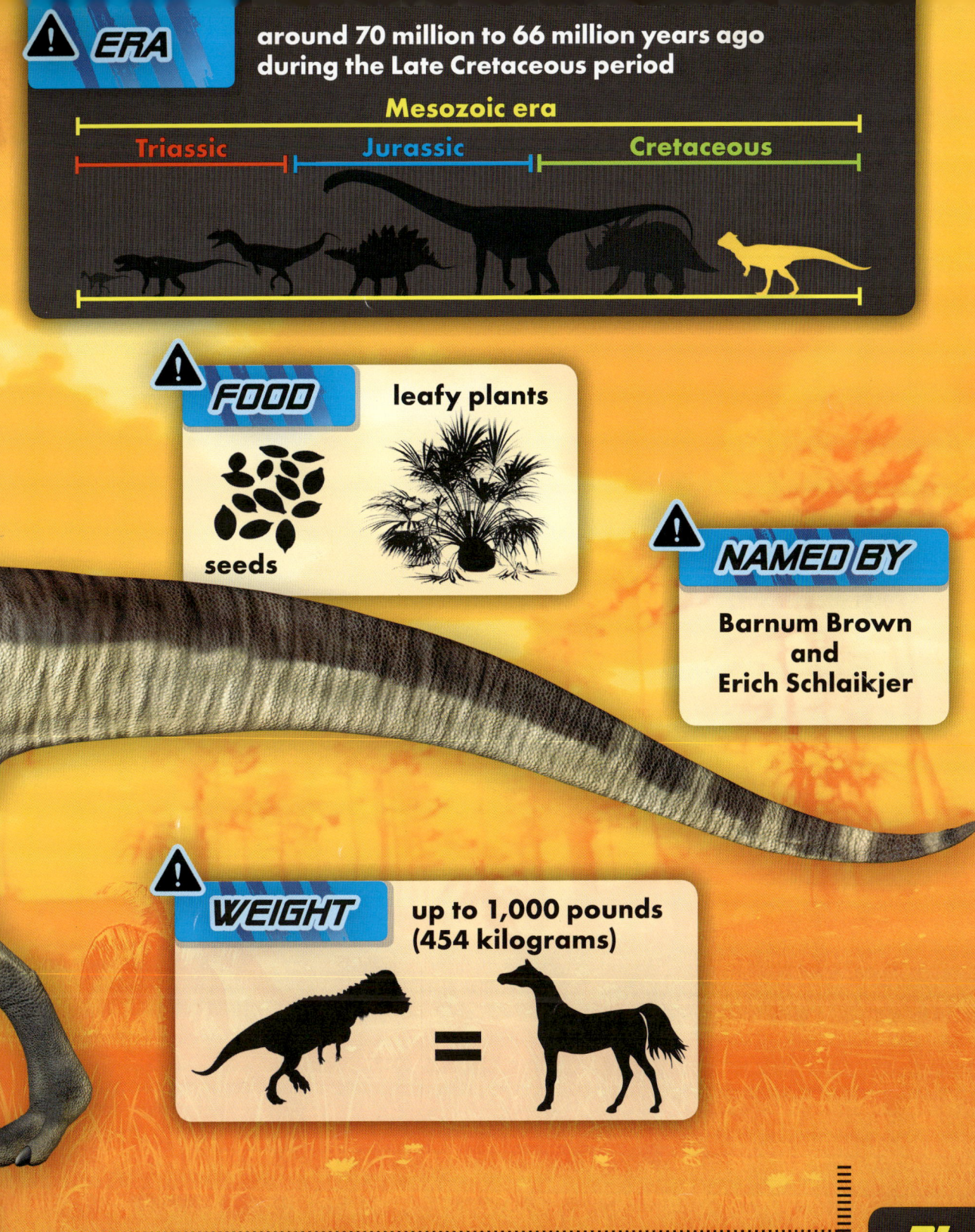

ERA
around 70 million to 66 million years ago during the Late Cretaceous period

Mesozoic era
Triassic | Jurassic | Cretaceous

FOOD
leafy plants
seeds

NAMED BY
Barnum Brown and Erich Schlaikjer

WEIGHT
up to 1,000 pounds (454 kilograms)

21

GLOSSARY

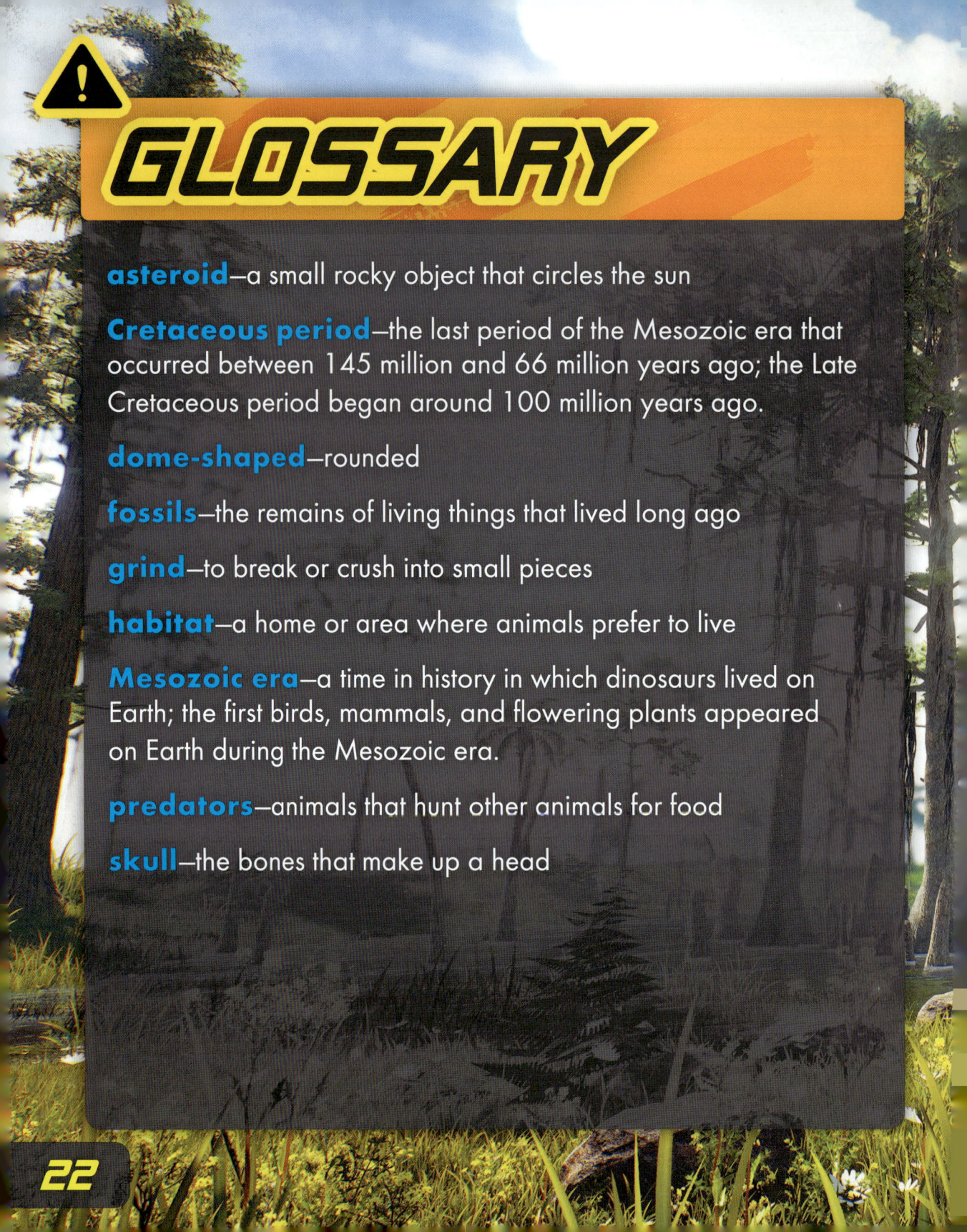

asteroid—a small rocky object that circles the sun

Cretaceous period—the last period of the Mesozoic era that occurred between 145 million and 66 million years ago; the Late Cretaceous period began around 100 million years ago.

dome-shaped—rounded

fossils—the remains of living things that lived long ago

grind—to break or crush into small pieces

habitat—a home or area where animals prefer to live

Mesozoic era—a time in history in which dinosaurs lived on Earth; the first birds, mammals, and flowering plants appeared on Earth during the Mesozoic era.

predators—animals that hunt other animals for food

skull—the bones that make up a head

TO LEARN MORE

AT THE LIBRARY

Pettiford, Rebecca. *Fossils*. Minneapolis, Minn.: Jump!, 2019.

Rathburn, Betsy. *Asteroid Belt*. Minneapolis, Minn.: Bellwether Media, 2023.

Sabelko, Rebecca. *Tyrannosaurus Rex*. Minneapolis, Minn.: Bellwether Media, 2020.

ON THE WEB

FACTSURFER

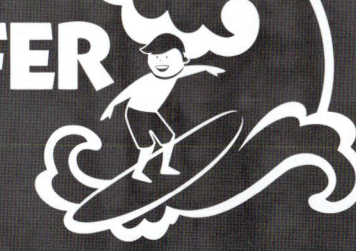

Factsurfer.com gives you a safe, fun way to find more information.

1. Go to www.factsurfer.com.
2. Enter "pachycephalosaurus" into the search box and click 🔍.
3. Select your book cover to see a list of related content.

INDEX

arms, 9
asteroid, 16, 17
beak, 10, 11
Canada, 18
dome, 4, 6, 7, 9, 19
eyes, 15
fights, 7
food, 10, 11, 13
fossils, 9, 18, 19
get to know, 20-21
habitat, 14, 17
Late Cretaceous period, 5
legs, 9
map, 5, 19

Mesozoic era, 5
name, 5
North America, 18
predators, 14, 15
pronunciation, 4
scientists, 7, 19
size, 6, 8, 9
skull, 18
spikes, 6, 7
teeth, 11, 12, 13
Tyrannosaurus rex, 14, 15
United States, 18
young, 9

The images in this book are reproduced through the courtesy of: James Kuether, front cover, pp. 4-5, 6-7, 8-9, 10-11, 11 (leafy plants), 11 (lizards), 12-13, 14-15, 16-17, 20-21; HQ3DMOD, p. 11 (seeds); AKKHARAT JARUSILAWONG, pp. 18-19.

24